TopReaders

Into the Unknown

Robert Coupe

Contents

People love to solve mysteries. They need to explore things and places that they do not know or understand. Many mysteries that puzzled people in earlier times have now been explained. But there are still questions that, even now, remain to be answered.

The First Americans

More than 15,000 years ago, ice covered the seas between Siberia and Alaska. Hunters followed herds of grazing animals across the land and ice. They moved south into North America. These people, who came from Asia all that time ago, became the earliest American Indians.

In early days, American Indians carried everything they owned as they moved across the land. They hunted animals with spears that had stone tips.

This map shows where people moved over ice from Siberia to Alaska.

Cerberus, a large, fierce dog with three heads, guarded the entrance to Hades so that no one could escape.

Journey to the Underworld

Ancient Greeks believed that dead people went to a place called Hades. To get there, they had to cross the River Styx. They needed to pay a coin to the man who took them across in a boat. The coin was buried with the dead person. If they did not have a coin, dead people could not get into Hades.

The Egyptian Way

When ancient Egyptian rulers died, they were buried with food and other goods they might need in their life after death.

Studying Medicine

In the early 1500s, doctors did not really understand the human body. Most believed what Claudius Galen, a doctor in ancient Rome, had written 1,400 years earlier. Galen studied animal bodies. He thought human bodies worked in the same way. As a result, he made many errors.

Andreas Vesalius worked in Padua, Italy, in the mid-1500s. He taught students how to cut up dead people to find out what really happened inside the human body.

Modern Medicine

For more than 100 years, doctors have used X-rays to inspect broken bones and other problems inside people's bodies.

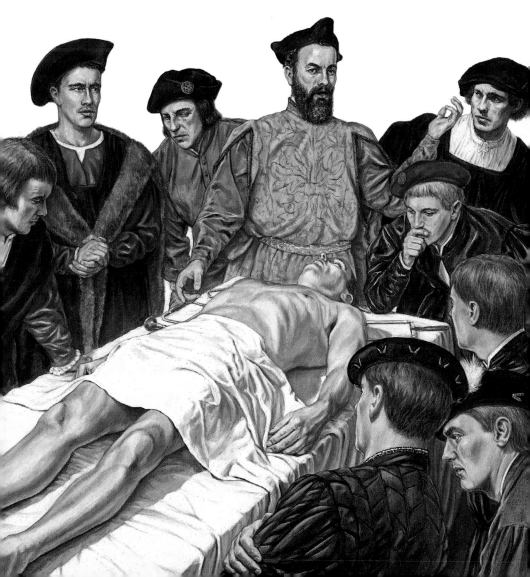

The Unknown Seas

People have sailed the seas for thousands of years.
In earlier days, sailors had no maps to guide them.
They used the sun and the stars to find their way.
Over the years, instruments were invented that helped
people at sea to navigate more easily and safely.

*Until the age of steamships, sailing ships
carried people on long ocean voyages.
Some used rowers as well as sails.*

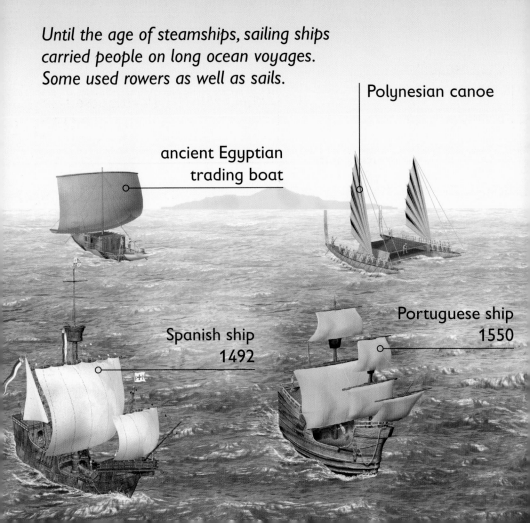

Polynesian canoe

ancient Egyptian
trading boat

Spanish ship
1492

Portuguese ship
1550

The Sextant

The sextant was invented in 1731. By using it, sailors could calculate their position accurately.

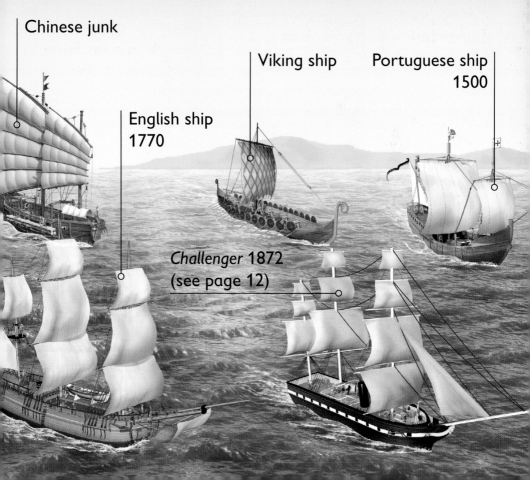

Chinese junk

English ship 1770

Viking ship

Portuguese ship 1500

Challenger 1872 (see page 12)

Under the Sea

In 1872, the sailing ship *Challenger* left England.
In the next four years, scientists on board studied
and brought back samples from
the deepest parts of the oceans.
They discovered many kinds
of plants and sea creatures.
They studied sea currents
and sea temperatures.

There were laboratories
on the Challenger, *where
scientists could investigate
the plants and animals they found.*

Fact File

Professor Wyville Thomson was the chief scientist on the *Challenger*. The scientists wrote 50 books about everything they found. Study of the oceans had really begun!

Dangerous Journeys

For centuries, sea explorers tried to find a way between the Atlantic and Pacific oceans along the northern coast of America. Many ships were lost in the icy waters. Finally, in 1906, the Norwegian explorer Roald Amundsen sailed through this "Northwest Passage."

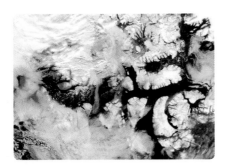

The Northwest Passage from the air.

In the 1500s and 1600s English and French ships tried to find the Northwest Passage. Many got trapped in ice. Sailors often died of scurvy *.*

Submersibles

Submersibles are small submarines. They can go deeper than larger submarines. They take scientists down to the ocean depths. Some submersibles are controlled by robots. They do not have people in them. These very small machines can reach places that larger submersibles cannot get to.

Alvin *is an American submersible. It can take people almost 15,000 feet (4,600 m) under the sea's surface.*

Jason Junior

Jason Junior is a robot submersible that is attached to *Alvin*. It can take photos in places where it is too dangerous for *Alvin* to go.

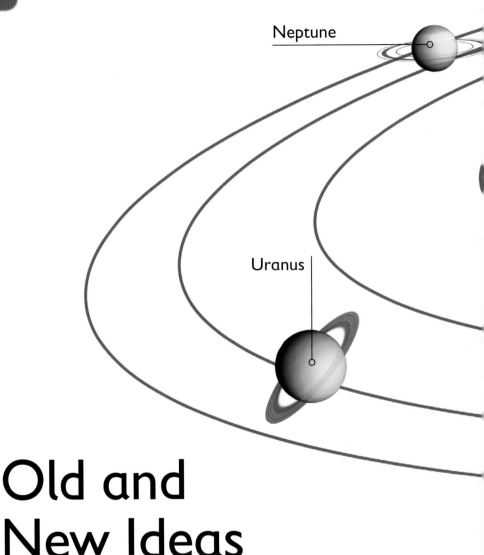

Neptune

Uranus

Old and New Ideas

We now know that Earth and other planets move around the Sun. But for many centuries people thought that Earth was the center of the universe. They believed that the Sun and everything else in the sky moved around our planet.

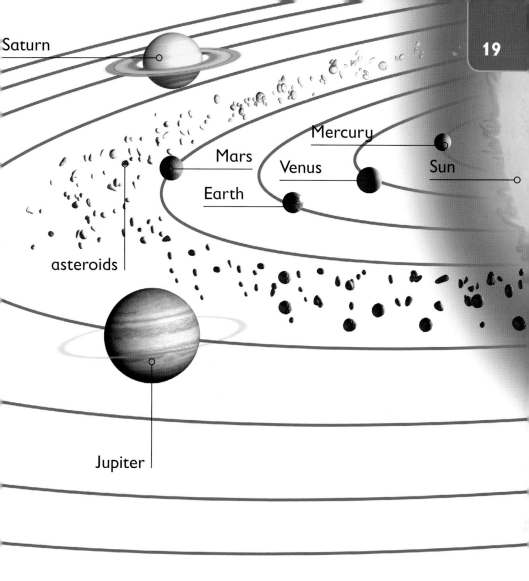

Saturn

Mercury

Mars

Venus

Sun

Earth

asteroids

Jupiter

The Sun is the center of our solar system. Earth and other planets, as well as dwarf planets and asteroids, all move in orbit around the Sun.

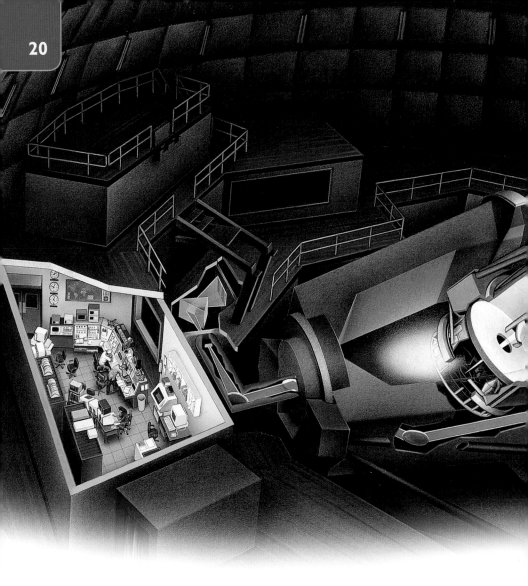

Space Telescopes

In 1609 Galileo Galilei used a telescope to look at the stars and planets. He was the first person to do this. Today, scientists look deep into space. They use huge telescopes in buildings called observatories.

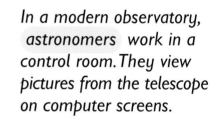

In a modern observatory, astronomers work in a control room. They view pictures from the telescope on computer screens.

Herschel's Telescope

William Herschel's telescope had a mirror 48 inches (1.2 m) across. In 1781, he was the first to see the planet Uranus. He studied the Milky Way galaxy.

Sometimes, astronauts need to leave their shuttle to make repairs or do other jobs. They must wear special space suits.

Fact File

The first traveler in space was a Russian dog called Laika. She was launched in 1957 in a satellite. In 1961, Yuri Gagarin went into space. He circled Earth for 108 minutes.

Space Shuttles

Space shuttles are aircraft that can fly into space. They can orbit Earth, but cannot travel farther. Astronauts in shuttles take new satellites into space. They also repair satellites that are already in orbit, or collect old satellites to bring back to Earth.

Space Stations

Space stations are buildings in space. People can live and work there for months at a time. The International Space Station (ISS) is still being built, but people are living there already. Sixteen countries are helping to build it.

solar panels

When it is completed in 2010, the ISS will be as big as a football field. Seven astronauts will live there at any one time.

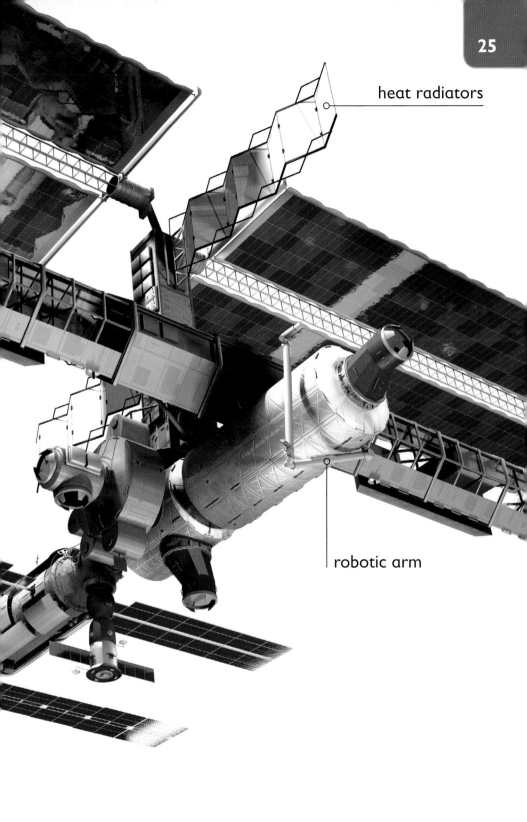

heat radiators

robotic arm

Space Probes

Space probes have taught us a lot about the planets. For more than 40 years, these robot machines have roamed our solar system. Some fly in orbit around a planet. Some land on planets and send back information about these planets' surfaces.

This space probe is approaching an asteroid.

In 2004, the probe Cassini *went into orbit around the distant planet Saturn. It took* Cassini *almost seven years to reach Saturn from Earth.*

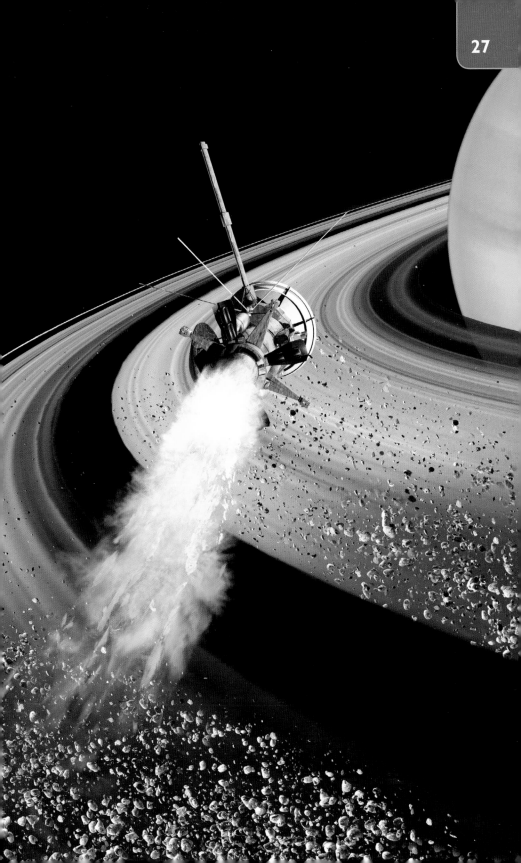

Looking for Life

There is life everywhere on Earth, even in hot, dark places deep in the oceans. Perhaps life does exist in other parts of our solar system. There may be an ocean beneath the ice that covers Europa, one of Jupiter's moons. And perhaps creatures live there.

Alien Life

Who knows if creatures like these might really exist in distant parts of the universe?

Scientists are working on a robot probe that will go to Europa. It will be designed to dive under the ice to find if anything lives there.

Quiz

Can you unscramble the words and match them with the right pictures?

SINICSA   NAILE

TESTNAX   BLSEUMISERB

Glossary

asteroids: rocky bodies, smaller than planets, that move in orbit around the Sun

astronauts: people who travel or work in space

astronomers: scientists who study the planets, the stars, and other parts of the universe

galaxy: a group of billions of stars, gas, and dust

laboratories: rooms where scientists do experiments or study things

navigate: to plan or direct a safe journey by sea or air

orbit: the path a body in space follows as it moves around another body, such as a star or a planet

satellites: spacecraft that travel around Earth or other planets. They send information to Earth.

scurvy: a disease caused by not eating enough fruit and vegetables that contain vitamin C

sextant: an instrument that sailors use to find out their position at sea

solar system: a group of planets and other natural bodies that move in orbit around a central star

submersibles: small craft, smaller than submarines, that can take people very deep under the sea

X-rays: rays that can pass through things that normal light rays cannot. They show images of people's bones and organs.

Index